J   Cumpian, Carlos.
811.54
CUMPIAN   Latino rainbow.

DATE			

5/09 x 22

LATINO RAINBOW

POEMS ABOUT LATINO AMERICANS

CARLOS CUMPIÁN ILLUSTRATED BY RICHARD LEONARD

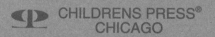

CHILDRENS PRESS®
CHICAGO

I WOULD LIKE TO THANK my family for their kind support and for lending me their "ears" as I formed each of these poems in their presence. I also want to thank my editors, Alice K. Flanagan and Cynthia Gallaher (my wife and a fellow bard who, being Irish, helped me find gold at the end of the rainbow). As my editors, I salute them for catching the poems thick with wrinkles and needing some stiff starch and a hot iron before appearing on the "stage" of the printed page. *Muchas gracías*, many thanks. — C.C.

IN DEDICATION to my mother Celia Martinez for her patience, love, and understanding, and to my beloved daughter Faviola.— R.L.

Library of Congress Cataloging-in-Publication Data

Cumpián, Carlos.
  Latino rainbow : poems about Latino Americans / by Carlos Cumpián
 : illustrated by Richard Leonard.
    p. cm. – – (Many voices, one song)
  Summary: Poems about Latino Americans such as César Chávez, Linda Ronstadt, Henry Cisneros, and Roberto Clemente.
  ISBN 0-516-05153-9
  1. Hispanic Americans--Biography--Juvenile poetry. 2. Hispanic Americans--History--Juvenile poetry. 3. Children's poetry, American. [1. Hispanic Americans--Poetry. 2. American poetry.]
I. Leonard, Richard, ill. II. Title. III. Series.
PS3553.U458L38 1994
811'.54--dc20   94-5069
                      CIP
                      AC

INTRODUCTION

In writing *Latino Rainbow*, it was my hope to offer a collection of poetry introducing the rich heritage of U.S. Latino culture and history. As a child in school, I never dreamed that one day my writing would help students become better acquainted with the Latinos and Latinas who have made a solid contribution to the growth of America. In those days, we Latinos were "invisible". Now we are on the horizon, like a rainbow — **A LATINO RAINBOW.**

NOTE TO READERS: For the best reading of *Latino Rainbow*, read each poem out loud standing up. In some cases, you might try practicing reading the poem twice. After discussing the poems and their meaning, you will find how much more "Latino literate" you have become.

TABLE OF CONTENTS

THE CALIFORNIA
RANCHEROS

Spain ruled
and mapped California
into little kingdoms since the 1770s,
with mission churches like adobe palaces,
until 1821, when a new sun rose
over upper and lower California,
becoming a province of the Republic of Mexico.

With Spain no longer setting aside
chunks of land to be used by Catholic friars,
the Mexicans tried to meet their people's needs
and turned mission lands into family farms
for native-born Californios.

Those first *ranchos* and *haciendas*
had their boundaries marked
by free men on horseback
using strong rope,
with piles of stone, desert brush,
or a notched tree trunk for markers.

The families Pacheco, Carillo, Pico,
and Vallejo became rich
selling sun-dried cattle hides
tied in bales for cargo ships
that sailed off to places that made
saddles, harnesses, coats, and shoes.

California's coast connected
money with cheap labor.
People from everywhere wanted to live there,
where weather laid a fertile carpet
for rich harvests.

After tasks were done,
in every rancho and village
there was time for fun—
piñatas, and songs at
birthdays, wedding dances,
and feasts on Catholic saints' days—
and you could expect a rodeo fiesta
even when it was time for cattle branding.

Yes, once the Californios strummed their guitars
and sang under a starlit sky,
their music rising from the ranchos
as the American pioneers,
eager for gold and land,
headed westward.

rancho—farm with mostly cattle ranching

hacienda—a large farm; an estate; property

piñata— a container filled with fruit, candies, money, used in a children's game

THE TREATY OF GUADALUPE HIDALGO

The sun hid behind a big dark cloud
when James Polk, the eleventh
U.S. president,
declared out loud
that Mexico would learn
a lesson for resisting with guns
America's plans for expansion.

Mexico was already wounded
a dozen years earlier
by English-speaking *Anglo Texicans*.
Wanting more land and black slaves
to work their farms and cotton plantations,
the Texicans launched a rebellion at the Alamo
to create the Texas "Lone Star" Republic.

Between May 1846 and February 1848,
the thorns of combat cut across
Mexico's northern horizon,
slashing towns, ranchos,
even missions in the desert.
The war stopped when a ship of U.S. Marines
stormed the Veracruz beach
as Hernan Cortés did centuries before
taking Mexico City.
And like Cortés's men, some marines learned that death
is the price of entry for those who dare touch *Moctezuma's* throne.

For Mexico, it ended in surrender
at a meeting in the village of Guadalupe Hidalgo,
where the treaty was signed covering America's respect
for Mexican rights and a massive land transfer.

The Treaty of Guadalupe Hidalgo
offered more than red earth Arizona
and the promise of sunbelt boom towns of
Tucson, Tempe, Phoenix, and Yuma.
After the gold rush in agricultural California,
rich crops of fresh grape, citrus, and vegetables
took root in fertile valleys providing work
to new communities — Sacramento,
San Francisco, Santa Barbara, San José —
all the way down to salty San Diego.

In mountainous Colorado, there's mile-high Denver,
popular Pueblo, college-town Boulder, and cattle-branded Durango.
And Nevada, at the time of the treaty, was large and mostly empty,
so who would have gambled on desert growth in Reno, Winnemucca,
Elko, and neon-flashy Las Vegas?
Utah was and is always *Ute* land, but in determination,
towns grew like rare trees in Cedar, Provo,
Ogden, and Mormon-founded Salt Lake City.

The treaty even redrew the borders of Texas
down to the *Rio Grande*, adding to America's map
cowboy towns Laredo and El Paso,
then to the gulf coast, where shippers sailed off
with crates of world cargo from Galveston
and hard-working Houston, Brownsville, and San Antonio.

The treaty helped create the American southwest,
where 80,000 Mexican people didn't cross the border
on February 2, 1848.
Instead, the border crossed over them,
making them the first *Chicanos* on that date.

Anglo Texicans—people living in the Mexican-controlled state of Texas in the 1800s
Moctezuma—name of two Aztec rulers of Mexico
Ute—a group of American Indians living in Utah, Colorado, Arizona and New Mexico
Rio Grande—the large river that forms the boundary between the United States and Mexico
Chicanos—Americans of Mexican ancestry

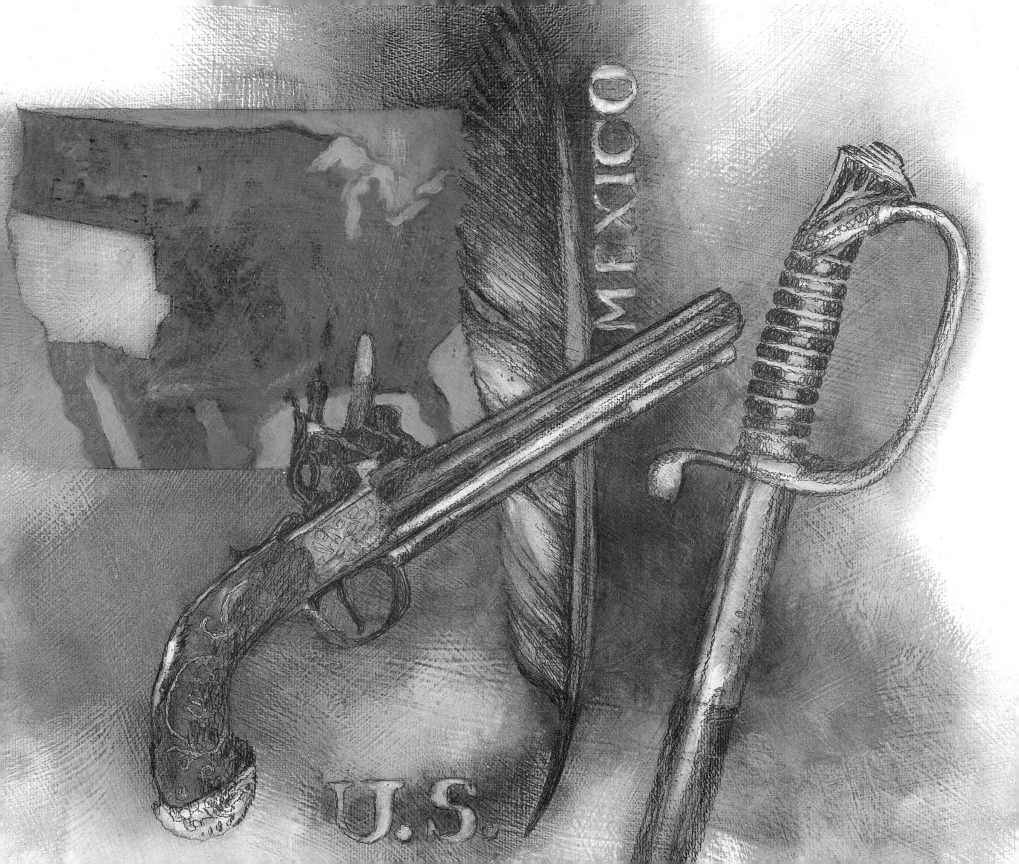

Who knew that Louis's small animal collection
under his family's front porch in Ithaca, New York,
would give wing to an artist's hand,
steady as an eagle's glide
through a mountain's current,
colorful as hummingbirds
in a field of flowers.

In Louis's pocket you might see a chickadee,
or in a cardboard box, a black-and-white skunk,
or bluejay feathers in a big jar.
His favorite book at the library was
John Audubon's *Birds of America*.
Each page inspired the young Louis
to take pictures with his mind
and draw the tiniest bird details
a hundred times to get it right.

He was happy to join the famous John Muir
on Florida and Alaska nature trips,
and in Texas, New Mexico,
the Bahamas, Saskatchewan,
Canadian Rockies, and sunny Yucatan,
he painted flocks of birds in the wild,
filling books that flew onto shelves
of homes, schools, and libraries.

LOUIS AGASSIZ FUERTES,
ARTIST AND NATURALIST

11

BERNARDO VEGA, TABAQUERO, ACTIVIST, MEMOIRIST

Bernardo Vega was not happy
when he left his warm home
and traveled by water with
thousands of others,
thousands of hopefuls who pulled out
from Puerto Rican harbors,
drawn by the magnet of jobs
in industrial America.

Bernardo Vega came on the *Coamo*.
He was one of the first
borinqueño arrivals to seek his fortune
just a small *coqui's* jump away
from New York's salty docks.
Bernardo was a skilled tradesman,
a maker of *puros*, a *tabaquero*,
forming cigars the old-fashioned way,
with leaves in hand, rolled by quick fingers.

Disappointed there were few jobs
for the others beyond this port of entry,
where the *"Lady with the Torch"* greets immigrants,
Vega brought Spanish-speaking workers together
to find a better way.

Bernardo Vega didn't quit.
He was able to make the fit
into life on the mainland
and wrote a book
about *barrio puertorriqueños'*
during years of struggle
in the "Iron Tower of Babel" —
New York City.

The Latino community should count itself lucky
that Bernardo Vega kept notes
of those early hard years
and how he made changes for the better
starting at the El Morito Cigar Factory on 86th Street.

Coamo—one of the first immigrant ships from Puerto Rico to the U.S.
coqui —a small frog that sings loudly at night; a folk symbol of Puerto Rico
borinqueños—another name for Puerto Ricans
puros—cigars
tabaquero—a tobacconist or cigar maker
"Lady with the Torch"—the Statue of Liberty in New York Harbor
barrio puertorriqueños—Puerto Ricans living in a Latino neighborhood

THE RONSTADT FAMILY OF TUCSON, A MUSICAL TRADITION

In the sixties, Linda Ronstadt
sang of a "different drum,"
but she wasn't first
in her family
to travel to the beat.
Grandfather Ronstadt, a Mexican-German
who settled in Tucson, Arizona,
created The Club Filarmonico,
a crazy mix of musicians that became
the town's leading orchestra.

And there was Aunt Luisa,
actress, folk dancer, and
classical musician,
who appeared in movies
and published Mexican folk songs,
like "Canciónes de mi Padre"
(Songs of My Father).

Linda's voice embraced American pop music
for many years,
but when she remembered
her father strumming a guitar,
playing the *huapangos* and *ranchereas*
on lazy Sunday afternoons,
her music changed once more to a different beat
as she gave color and voice
to "Canciónes de mi Padre"
throughout Spanish-speaking America.

huapangos—songs having nonsense verses
ranchereas—songs about the romantic behavior of men and women

The special Alvarez clan
heard the call of science,
each in his own way.
Take Luis's father, an American medical doctor
at the famous Mayo Clinic,
and Luis's grandfather, who left his home in Cuba
to become a government doctor
in the Kingdom of Hawaii,
or even Luis's son, who loved dinosaurs,
became a geologist,
and now works rocks and soil
with chisels and hammers.

And what about Luis,
born in San Francisco,
a student of physics,
who studied the small, invisible pieces
that make up the big pieces
of our whole world.
Luis found a radar beam so narrow
it could guide airplanes lost in fog
safely to the ground.

Someone said Luis loved doing
"what everyone else found impossible."
Yes, he found magic in numbers,
and mathematics made things happen
he could barely name.
So when the atomic bomb, that he
and other scientists helped create,
filled the Hiroshima air
with blasts of fierce fire and radiation,
a mushroom cloud of smoke,
he found words for that line of numbers,
for the addition and subtraction with an awful outcome—
"terrible weapon!"

LUIS ALVAREZ,
PHYSICIST,
NOBEL PRIZE WINNER

Sergeant Macario Garcia came home
from World War II to Texas,
wearing around his collar
the Congressional Medal of Honor.
He stopped at the Oasis Café
to enjoy a cup of coffee, but was told,
"We don't serve no Mexies in here."

Was this a just reward for Mexican-Americans
who have served their country?
And why could white veterans get medical help
while some brown and black couldn't?
Texan Latinos cried out when
a *raza* soldier who died in battle
was denied a resting place
by an *Anglo* undertaker
refusing to bury his remains.

In response, Dr. Hector Perez Garcia,
veteran combat surgeon from Corpus Christi,
put together an organization—
the American GI Forum—
to help Mexican-American veterans
get what is rightfully theirs
during war and peace.

raza—any person who shares Native American and Spanish heritage
Anglo—English – speaking Americans or whites

DR. HECTOR PEREZ GARCIA, DOCTOR AND CIVIL RIGHTS ORGANIZER

CUBAN REFUGEES

Fidel Castro seized
the baseball and sugarcane fields,
the department stores, Havana's hotels, and American-owned factories.
Yes, Castro seized Cuba from *Batista*,
on this we can agree,
but why did the doctors, lawyers, and dentists
take to boats and go to sea?

Their float to freedom wasn't far,
but could be dangerous to travel,
100 miles to southern Florida, U.S.A.
amid storms, sharks, and capsized cruisers.

Miami, once a Florida city on its way down,
was now a New Havana on its way up again
because determined people started
new business, new banking, new construction,
and seized new opportunity
in both English and Spanish.
Welcome ¡bienveñido!
new Cuban amigos.

Batista—two-time president of Cuba

RITCHIE VALENS,
SINGER AND SONGWRITER

Some say he was too young
when he stepped into
the American Legion Hall,
guitar slung over his shoulder.

But when Ritchie Valens sang,
there was something
timeless in his voice,
a sound that spanned the decades
to the Mexican beat of *"La Bamba."*

Some say he was too young
on the night he stepped aboard the small plane
that carried record breakers
Buddy Holly, The Big Bopper, and Ritchie Valens
over to the flip side of this life,
leaving a legacy of rock and roll,
and tears in some eyes.

"La Bamba"—a traditional wedding dance song in Mexican folklore

Baile-bamba
baile-samba
baile-mambo
dancers go, go, go —
Have *merengue*, will travel
across the night club floor.

You might be making people
cha-cha-cha to music in
Chicago or Mexico City,
San Juan or Honolulu,
far from your training grounds of the
Palladium Theater in New York,
where going to the top meant
raining on your *timbales*
four times a week
a thunderous danceable storm.
It was after music studies in Cuba
that you joined other masters
of the urban Afro-Latino-*Caribeño* sound,
matching beat-for-beat energy
with the leaders: Mario Banza,
Novo Morales and, of course,
Frank "Machito" Guillo
to perform before Blacks,
Latinos, and Whites who
would venture into the night,
swayed by the power inside
your Puerto Rican decorated drums,
sizzling *salsa* compositions transforming
live audiences across the world's seven continents.

Since you were a boy,
your *guaguanco* spirit has been burning
and churning your rhythmic hands,
expressed on the side of an empty coffee can,
or across the bridge connecting to Manhattan,
helping you become the "king of the drums"
whom we have loved for a weekend
or for all fifty years.

Because of your commitment to music,
beating praises for bamba-samba, and the mambo,
katapán-tum, katapán-tum, Ti-to Ti-to Puen-te,
making powerful party music for half a century,
whenever a *bembe*-slapping conga meets you Tito,
an island sun shines in every Puerto Rican soul.

baile—to dance
merengue—a dance played with a double-headed drum
timbales—drums
Caribeño—Caribbean person
salsa—spicy Latino music
guaguanco—Afro-Cuban form of music and dance linked to a type of rumba
bembe—A term referring to an Afro-Cuban ceremony, using drums

TITO PUENTE, MUSICIAN

THE NEORICAN POETS / NUYORICAN POETS

Somos los poetas. We are the poets, the Neorican Poets.
Our poems have been and always will be
proudly performed before live audiences in the Big City.
Sure, we write books and publish magazines,
and as far as new poems —
we have a thousand waiting in the wings.
We're totally current.
Find us on cable or video cause we're popping to a hot congero beat,
using English and Spanish at your window or nest
on the best CD speakers carrying our words through your ears
to that sweet island heart in your royal chest.

Now people ask us, "Where do you get your ideas?"
"How long does it take you guys to finish a poem?"
Ideas call us on the brain phone, some ideas are faxed in our sleep.
No lo creo?
You better believe it little brother, do you scan my zone?
Ideas can come from just hanging around,
tuned in to young and old *barrio* souls,
walking and winging it on streets, schools, and parks.
We get our education from the community
as it goes about working, playing, dreaming, or suffering
in the daylight and the dark.

Looking for inspiration can be
as easy as seeing faces in New York.
A poem's spark might leap out at us from a matchbook cover,
an album jacket, billboards, or wall murals in four-story color.
When you're a Neorican poet, you have teachers like
Piri Thomas, Miguel Piñero,
Lucky CienFuegos, Sandra Maria Esteves,
Miguel Algarin, Pedro Pietri,
Tato Laviera, Jose-Angel Figueroa,
Victor Hernandez Cruz, and dozens more
who make poetry to share on the page, stage, or air.

We live in New York — Nueva York— the big apple,
and the *manzana* of *mañana* looks Puerto Rican,
so we won't stop writing about our love
building a new culture with its deep tradition.
We will take forever to do our poems.
Somos los poetas. We are the poets, the Nuyorican Poets.

Somos los poetas—"We are the poets."
No lo creo?—"You don't believe me?"
barrio—a Latino neighborhood
manzana—an apple
mañana—tomorrow

CÉSAR CHÁVEZ,
FARM WORKER
ORGANIZER

No machine can harvest
delicate leafy lettuce,
the low, hidden melons,
the oval cradles of
newborn almonds,
or those green and purple
clusters of coolness—grapes.

It takes a mindful hand
to reach for and pull close
such plenty for the orchard owner.

But why, asked César Chávez,
in this land of California dreams,
must our children suffer
the nightmare of pesticides
and their parents wake without rights or decent wages.

Tractors have barns,
animals have stalls,
but the migrant worker
has nowhere to lay his head.
Where's Eden in these gardens
of San Joaquin Valley?

And the hands that picked the grapes,
joined in number,
rallied and held up posters,
and the feet that trod
down field rows,
led by César,
marched together.

He gave new dignity to the farmworker,
a strong union to lead the way.
Will you join with César Chávez's friends,
like Dolores Huerta,
in making things better today?

It's a long way
from Puerto Rico's sandlots
to the diamond fields of Pittsburgh,
farther still for a black Latino ballplayer
who barely spoke English
in the 1950s.

He seemed the long shot,
a small, skinny boy
who made his own baseballs
from burlap, string, and tape.
Who'd guess he'd hit three thousand
in the major leagues one day?

But it was clear to those who saw
his steady hands and on-target pitches,
and as his eyes turned toward the clouds,
how he'd swing, hit, and hurl the ball
over his neighborhood's walls.

By the 1960s World Series,
hard-hitting Roberto Clemente
became a Caribbean hurricane in human form,
and fellow ball players and fans
saw him whirl on to earn the title
of *Most Valuable Player*,
and take his place in the Hall of Fame.

Fans who saw him from the stands
will remember how he caught the ball
with both feet off the ground
and found the fastest, shortest
distance between three bases and home.

ROBERTO CLEMENTE,
BASEBALL HALL OF FAMER

CARLOS A. CORTEZ, CHICANO ARTIST AND POET

He drew like a stone-age child holding a red pencil,
filling his sunny bedroom wall with the
neighbor's two loose cats, fat crazy circles and wavy whiskers.
Carlos drew wild pictures until mama caught him,
then she taught him drawing would bring him attention.

Later, Carlos left his old Milwaukee town,
traveled with his wife Marianna before moving
to Chicago, soon they had jobs and a home.
Slowly, their place became a gallery for posters,
paintings, and Mexican folk art pieces.
In their basement, Carlos feeds his *gato negro*,
whose paw prints leave colored ink for new walls.

Carlos embraced many art traditions.
He learned about famous wood printmakers.
They influenced him like real friends.
Carlos wanted to share his cultural treasure
and joined muralist and poet *compañeros*
in Chicago's *El Movimiento Artistico Chicano*.

His work and travel experiences have
helped him write pages of poetry.
Carlos, like you, has wishes
for a healthy planet, safe for
people of all ages.

Now, Carlos knows most jobs will come and go,
but a "career" as a community artist and poet
really gets deep in your bones.

el gato negro—the black cat, Carlos Cortez's printing press
El Movimiento Artistico Chicano—an arts and poetry group in Chicago, Illinois
compañeros—companions

Behind the song stands the singer,
behind the singer, the person,
behind the person, the spirit,
and the will to make change.

The air fills with her music,
and how sweet the sound,
as crowds are awed by
"Gracias a la Vida" and
"Amazing Grace."

And she picks each note by hand,
plays them from her heart,
and we find that her folk music
is heard across the land.

Her guitar's a lightning rod
catching all the change,
and her voice ascends
a multi-colored mountain range.

In between the music chords
stand all the people
who could learn
to share the earth
"in peace, in peace,"
Joan Baez sings,
"brothers and sisters,
let's hold hands."

Amid the gunfire,
the injustice, and division,
we join her singing,
and a new world
comes alive!

"Gracias a la Vida"—"Thanks to Life"

JOAN BAEZ, FOLK SINGER AND CIVIL RIGHTS ACTIVIST

REIES LÓPEZ TIJERINA, SPANISH LAND GRANTS ORGANIZER

Reies López Tijerina,
the human tiger from Texas,
roamed the Southwest's hills and valleys,
hunting for justice for the humble *mestizo* families
who once owned farms, pastures, and ranches
in New Mexico's *Tierra Amarilla*.

Reies was embraced by the people, and together
they formed the *Alianza de los Pueblos Libres*
to regain the Brazos, Chamas, and Sangre de Cristo mountains
and all the land north of the Rio Grande.

Reies "growled" at how poor Indians and mestizos lived
in run-down schools and houses so close to red apple orchards,
lush green meadows, blue spruce and piñon pine forests,
mountains, cold trout streams, and grazing pastures,
all for the rich who live as fast as shooting stars.

Reies's beliefs lit fires in the hearts of *Indio-Hispanos*,
his cries even moved the younger of *Aztlan's* Chicanos
to be strong like their ancestors who had survived
hunger, fierce storms, and even U.S. General Stephen Kearny,
who in 1848 made New Mexico occupied American territory.

Reies challenged both the Anglos and their handy *"Tio Tacos,"*
who turned rural folks into cute tourist attractions,
mere shadows in their own land,
trapped like sad genies in forgotten, dusty bottles.

Reies's free Pueblo men and women broke the bottles of confinement
by protesting both Mexican and American nations
who refused to help them find the rightful owners
of Spanish land-granted Tierra Amarilla.

Was this the "Land of Enchantment,"
where the families of Baca, Lujan, Gallego, Martinez, Serrano, and Silva—
all decendants of early stonecutters, shepherds, and soldiers
of Santa Fe's mission — could now be treated
as no good troublemakers for wanting what was rightfully theirs?

On June 5, 1967, the Alianza entered history,
arresting corrupt officials in a "courthouse raid."
Then the U.S. army and police went on a full-alert search
in the angry New Mexican hills,
where the Alianza had posted *"Tierra O Muerte,"*
their rallying cry to unwanted outsiders.

After days of tanks and bloodhounds,
Reies and some of his fighters
were captured, put on trial, and sent to prison.
This is the price they paid for believing, like *Zapata*,
in a justice-seeking dream,
wanting the land to belong to those who work and respect it.

Today, because of the Alianza's actions,
millions of Chicanos from California to Chicago can say
"Long live Tijerina and his call for the land!"

mestizo—a person of mixed European and American Indian ancestry
Tierra Amarilla—area of Northern New Mexico
Alianza de los Pueblos Libres—Alliance of Free City States
Indio-Hispanos—People of both Indian and Spanish heritage
Aztlan—the Aztec's sacred place of origin
Tio Tacos—people who are traitors
Zapata—Indian leader in Mexico who fought to gain land for his people
"Tierra O Muerte"—"Land of Death"

ANTONIA COELHO NOVELLO,
U.S. SURGEON GENERAL

Our country's first
Puerto Rican surgeon general
did not take a kicked-back,
chillin-to-a-slow-freeze,
mellow approach
to helping her fellow Americans,
especially those of Latino heritage.

She was on the job from day one,
helping solve America's many health problems;
from high blood pressure,
diabetes, breast and lung cancer,
to drug addiction, AIDS, TB,
and sickle cell anemia.
Sometimes, she helped school children
get their needed vaccine shots.

Antonia Coelho Novello was involved,
working with her dedicated team
to be sure each ethnic American community
had its place at planning tables
where the president and other leaders gather.

Antonia Coelho Novello traveled
to every corner of this big land,
keeping score on what more
could be done in this war against disease,
as our nation's leading doctor,
the U.S. surgeon general.

My parents couldn't grow
enough food to feed us,
and nothing was left to sell.
My daddy said the seeds and land
had become hard to afford
but the villagers got together
to see if they could buy more.

Acre by acre, our cycle of
planting, weeding,
harvesting, and going to market
was being broken
while rich banana growers
put up fences across the river.
Our sweet land became smaller
as thick green groves were cut down
for cattle ranchers; soon
they wanted our fields as well.

One Sunday after church, I took a long walk
to think about an answer to our problems.
As I looked up, the sky mocked my hunger,
with fluffy cloud tortillas drifting overhead,
far out of reach of *mi pueblo*.

At my feet, soldier ants dragged
our last dried corn kernels and straw
to store in underground chambers.
When I returned home,
it was decided we were leaving
for *el norte*.

Now we live in the U.S.A. where it's often cold,
Where people pronounce our names
with robot-like faces
speaking in slow motion.
It seems like only a few understand
the meaning of our songs,
*"Una rama es muy delgada,
y muy facil pa quebra."*

CENTRAL AMERICAN REFUGEES: GUATEMALAN, EL SALVADORIAN, AND NICARAGUAN

Six months ago,
another Guatemalan family
left its small highland village.
Look into their dark brown eyes
and see a hurt they still carry
for those kidnapped and killed—
village elders who complained
about the ranchers and the rich.

Our people have become refugees
because of strong earthquakes, high floods,
diseased water, or no rain;
because mean people
took control and wanted to rule
without caring about clinics,
food markets, or even schools.

That's why we have come to the United States,
refugees from far away—
Central Americans—struggling
landino, mestizo, and Indian people,
who need to be treated
as you would treat your friends.

mi pueblo—my people or community
el norte—the north, or the U.S.
Una rama es muy delgada...—means "one little branch is very thin and so easy to break off"
landino—a Spanish-speaking person living in Guatemala

40

HENRY CISNEROS, POLITICAL LEADER

Did you know a political leader
can at times be like a
long-distance runner?
If I asked you the name of someone
who ran from neighborhood to neighborhood,
talking about what's good for the people,
would the name be —Henry Cisneros?

Cisneros carries the cause
under full-time pressure,
always keeping a keen vision
on how to measure what
people want and people need.

He started training early,
working mind and body
under his parents' wise
direction and reflections
de lo bueño,
growing strong from
years of study.

He's brown-skinned and bilingual,
a man on track, finding solutions
for those who have been
left out.

Did young Cisneros,
of ol' San Antone, ever know what bigger
doors would be opening for him
after city council and mayor?

Henry Cisneros,
a practical man with many
titles and skills,
has his head in the stars
and his feet on the ground.

de lo bueño—what is correct or good

ELLEN OCHOA, FIRST LATINA ASTRONAUT

Did Ellen know, during her childhood flute lessons,
that she'd play classical music
miles above our blue-green, marble-earth home?

Ellen sails through the ionosphere, where
carbon dioxide, nitrogen, and oxygen are recycled,
then piped-in fresh as a new song
so the brave astronauts can get
their scientific jobs done.

From inside the shuttle,
Ellen Ochoa, America's first
Latina astronaut, flies far above hot volcanoes,
ice-tipped mountains, and nearer the pearl moon
that seems to smile over her native California.

Ellen checks the payload,
dreams of future space exploration,
hears music in the numbers,
feels the rhythm to the reasons
as her team prepares and practices
for trips far out in orbit.

GLOSSARY

acre An area equal to 4,840 square yards.

adobe (u DOH bee) Made of a brick formed of clay and straw and dried in the sun.

amigo Friend.

ascend Climb.

Audubon, John James (1785-1851) Ornithologist (scientist specializing in the study of birds) and artist.

bale Large bundle of goods, usually closely pressed and tied.

Beat Referring to writers who were part of a movement of the 1950s that rejected standard middle-class values.

bienvenido Welcome.

Big Apple New York City.

bilingual Able to speak two languages well.

boomtown A town that is growing fast in population and importance.

burlap Coarse cloth used especially to make bags and sacks.

Caribbean From the area of the Caribbean Sea: its Central and South American coasts or its islands.

chamber Room; enclosed space.

Chicano American of Mexican ancestry.

churn Cause to move forcefully.

commitment Dedication, devotion, loyalty.

confinement The state of having one's movement limited; imprisonment.

corrupt Dishonest.

cultural Having to do with the knowledge, art, and history of a people.

current Air that moves continuously in one direction.

cycle Events that are repeated, always in the same order.

diabetes A disease in which the patient has a high level of sugar in the blood.

different drum A call or interest that differs from what others hear or feel. From *Walden* by Henry David Thoreau: "... he hears a different drummer."

Eden Paradise; happiness.

embrace Include; take up gladly; welcome; cherish.

ethnic Describing a group identified by their (or their ancestors') country of origin.

fiesta Festival, celebration.

filarmonico Philharmonic; devoted to or loving music.

forum Something or someplace for open discussion about matters of importance.

friar (FRY'r) A member of a Roman Catholic religious order.

geologist Scientist who specializes in the study of soil, rocks, and minerals.

46

grove A carefully tended stand of trees, especially fruit or nut.

Hiroshima City in Japan destroyed in World War II (August 6, 1945) by the first atomic bomb.

ionosphere A region of the earth's atmosphere, extending 30 to 250 miles (50 to 400 kilometers) above the surface.

Kearny, Stephen Watts (KAR nee) (1794-1848) American general in the Mexican War who commanded the Army of the West, took Santa Fe and Los Angeles, and later served as the military governor of California.
keen Sharp.

legacy What is passed down from one's ancestors; includes property and such things as knowledge, traditions, arts, and beliefs.
lightning rod Anything that acts like a lightning rod, attracting powerful feelings and emotions.

massive Large; broad in extent.
Mayo Clinic Clinic founded in Rochester, Minnesota, by the Mayo brothers.
memoirist Person who keeps an account (a memoir) of his or her personal experiences.
mindful Careful.
Muir, John James (1838-1914) Naturalist who called for the creation of national parks.

Nobel Prize International prize awarded for outstanding accomplishments in six areas.

payload In a spacecraft, the part that carries the crew and its equipment.
physics A science that deals with light, motion, sound, heat, electricity, and force.

Rio Grande The large river that forms the boundary between the United States and Mexico.

San Antone San Antonio, Texas.
San Joaquin Valley (waw KEEN) a region in central California with rich farmland.
sickle cell anemia A disease in which the patient's red blood cells are shaped like a sickle; found usually in people of African descent.

sunbelt Southern and southwestern United States.
Surgeon General The chief officer in the U.S. Public Health Service.
Tower of Babel Tower described in the Old Testament. Its builders were trying to reach heaven, but construction was halted because they could no longer understand one another.
trod (past tense of *tread*) Walked on.
Tucson (TU sawn) A city in southeast Arizona.

venture Go, despite possible danger.

ABOUT THE AUTHOR

Born in San Antonio, Texas, Carlos Cumpián spent his formative years in the U.S. Southwest. His love of poetry began when he was a sophomore in high school. He started writing at the age of twenty and published his first poem in a small Chicago-based Chicano cultural journal called *Abrazo* when he was twenty-three. Since then, his work has been published in numerous magazines, newspapers, and poetry collections. His first book of poetry, *Coyote Sun*, was published in 1990. Carlos Cumpián enjoys reading his poetry at schools, libraries, and cultural events in Chicago, Illinois, where he currently resides, and also gives poetry readings throughout the United States and Mexico.

ABOUT THE ILLUSTRATOR

Born in Florida of Cuban heritage, Richard Leonard is a graduate of Pratt Institute in Brooklyn, New York. He has produced murals, book illustrations, and several works in galleries and now works primarily as a freelance illustrator. His illustrations for *Latino Rainbow* were created in oil on canvas, capturing the richness and diversity of the Latino culture.

ACKNOWLEDGMENTS

Project Editor: Alice Flanagan
Design and Electronic Page Composition:
    PCI Design Group, San Antonio, Texas
Engraver: Liberty Photoengravers
Printer: Lake Book Manufacturing, Inc.
Photograph of Carlos Cumpián: © Virginia Boyle